AMAZON

FBA

BOOK DESCRIPTION

Amazon is no doubt a multi-billion dollar enterprise that has built its reputation as a global online marketplace where both consumers and suppliers interact for business. Budding entrepreneurs have made it big by starting off their enterprises on Amazon. You are not an exception.

This book is a guide that is specifically tailored to provide you with practical hand-on information to enable you launch your passive income business enterprise on Amazon.

The guide begins by explaining to you, in a beginner-approach, what Amazon FBA is and how to create a Private Label that you can sell using FBA. It goes on to the next logical step – setting up Amazon seller account, by showing you how to open and set up your Amazon seller account.

Choosing a niche that can enable you to make a six-figure passive income is not just a gamble. You have to apply both science (logic) and art (creativity) plus a bit of gut and passion to come up with the niche which will define the nature of your enterprise. This guide teaches you how to choose your niche so as to give you a great chance at achieving a income of $1000 to $100000 per month (or more)– given you put in the required time and effort.

After choosing a niche, the next logical step is to choose your supplier for your private label. The guide provides you with criteria for choosing a supplier and where to find your potential supplier so that you can successfully launch your private label.

Once you have established your niche, decided on products to sell and found a supplier for your private label, you can now comfortably embark on setting up your listing (storefront, in a traditional sense). How you set up your listing determines whether buyers will be encouraged to buy your products or not. Thus, it is important to get it right, first time. Thanks to information provided in this guide, you can't simply go wrong.

Unlike the traditional brick-and-mortar storefront where you use sign posts, directional posts and human guides to direct potential customers to your place, you need a different approach as this can't work out online. Search Engine Optimization (SEO) using keywords is the way to achieve this online. This guide provides you with hands-on practical steps on how you find and use keywords for SEO so that you can drive traffic to your product brand and quickly get initial positive reviews.

To scale up your FBA private label business and propel your passive income to higher levels, you need to take advantage of technology. Luckily, there is a good number of great FBA automation tools that can rocket-propel your passive income into the clouds and beyond.

Enjoy your reading!

ABOUT THE AUTHOR

George Pain is an entrepreneur, author and business consultant. He specializes in setting up online businesses from scratch, investment income strategies and global mobility solutions. He has built several businesses from the ground up, and is excited to share his knowledge with readers.

DISCLAIMER

Contents

BOOK DESCRIPTION..2

ABOUT THE AUTHOR 4

DISCLAIMER 5

INTRODUCTION 8

WHAT IS AMAZON FBA AND PRIVATE LABELING? 9

SETTING UP AN AMAZON SELLER ACCOUNT?....................23

Getting started - Preparing to register 23

Opening up your Amazon seller account........................ 28

Setting up your seller profile 28

Encouraging feedback 29

HOW TO CHOOSE YOUR NICHE 30

Know your situation 30

Great sources of product ideas 37

HOW TO CHOOSE YOUR SUPPLIER 39

Criteria for choosing your supplier 40

Where to source supplier info 41

HOW TO SETUP YOUR LISTING 42

Listing sections/components 42

How to list a product 46

KEYWORD OPTIMIZATION OF YOUR LISTING..................... 48

Understanding Amazon's Algorithm....................................... 48

How to carry out thorough keyword research 50

How to optimize your listing content.......................................55

BRANDING YOUR PRODUCTS 60

Brand development 60

Amazon Brand Registry (ABR) – this is optional 66

Amazon's Enhanced Brand Content (EBC) – this is optional .67

DRIVING TRAFFIC AND GETTING INITIAL REVIEWS 68

Driving traffic from Amazon ecosystem into your listing........69

Getting initial reviews..74

AUTOMATING THE PROCESS 76

Processes that you can automate..76

FBA Automation Tools 80

CONCLUSION 87

INTRODUCTION

Amazon is the world's biggest online marketplace for consumer goods. It is a great place where enterprising minds can start off to build private label empires by leveraging the Amazon FBA global logistics infrastructure to their advantage. Unfortunately, many would-be global entrepreneurs lack relevant information about Private Labeling and Amazon FBA.

This book presents a practical hands-on guide specifically tailored to provide relevant information to potential entrepreneurs about Amazon FBA and Private Labeling so that they can be inspired to start off, launch their enterprise and succeed in making six-figure passive income streams – in a shorter time, with lower financial resources and effort.

If you are a budding entrepreneur or have a need to boost your income; "Amazon FBA Private Label BluePrint to Build a Profitable Business or Passive Income Stream for Beginners" is the right guide to find out how.

Keep reading!

WHAT IS AMAZON FBA AND PRIVATE LABELING?

Amazon FBA and Private Labeling are some of the most popular words mentioned by entrepreneurs seeking to do business on Amazon. This is so because Amazon FBA has transformed the way global business is being conducted.

What does FBA stand for?

FBA is an acronym for Fulfillment by Amazon.

What is Fulfillment?

The term 'Fulfillment' is commonly used in merchandize businesses by vendors when it comes to dealing with orders. The Order is either 'fulfilled' or 'unfulfilled'. A fulfilled Order is one where the goods are delivered as per the Order and all its terms met including invoicing, billing and payment. Unfulfilled Order is an order that has not yet been acted upon or it is not completed.

Thus, in a more technical sense, fulfillment can be defined as the whole process of receiving, packaging and delivering as per the Order.

Fulfillment is commonly applied in ecommerce.

Why outsource fulfillment?

Like any other service that one outsources, the following are basic guiding criteria for outsourcing fulfillment service;

- When it becomes more expensive to render the service in-house

- When it becomes more productive to focus on the core functions and thus the need to outsource non-core functions

- When the level of expertise required to render the service is so complex that it cannot be economically met in-house

- When the scale of operation is too big to be met in-house e.g. international delivery networks that requires extensive logistics infrastructure

What does an ordinary fulfillment entail?

Basically, fulfillment, though depends on custom contractual terms, encompasses the following;

- Warehousing (storage of goods)

- Order processing (including re-ordering)

- Delivery (including shipping)

- Returns and exchanges

However, fulfillment can be end-to-end, meaning that the fulfillment company carries out entire process. In addition to the above processes, an end-to-end fulfillment has the following;

- Billing

- Payment processing (Credit-card)

- Call-center services (customer service support)

What is actually Fulfillment by Amazon?

Fulfillment by Amazon (FBA) simply means letting Amazon fulfill an Order from your customer on your behalf. In essence, it is outsourcing your fulfillment service/function to Amazon. Amazon FBA is essentially an end-to-end fulfillment service that takes charge of;

- Warehousing

- Order processing

- Billing

- Returns and exchanges

- Payment processing

- Customer service support

How does Amazon FBA work?

Fulfillment by Amazon works through the following steps;

Step 1: Deliver your product to Amazon (via your Private Label supplier)

Step 2: Amazon stores your products in its inventory (thus undertakes basic inventory management)

Step 3: Customers buy your product (via the Amazon product page)

Step 4: Amazon picks and packs the product on your behalf

Step 5: Amazon delivers the product to your customer (including shipping)

Step 6: Amazon bills the customer and receives payment on your behalf

Step 7: Amazon channels payment to your bank account

What is private labeling?

Labeling refers to uniquely branding an item. Private labeling thus refers to uniquely branding an already existing product so that it appears as a unique product from you. For example, you can buy a plain T-shirt from a supplier and brand your name or logo on it. This becomes your private label of the T-shirt.

Why private labeling?

- Private labeling allows you to create your own unique brand – This helps to create a unique image recognition, marketing identity and customer loyalty

- High level of customization to meet the needs of a specific market niche – As a private label owner, you are able to make custom specifications, including product name, description, logo and contacts

- Greater autonomy and control – Control over branding, marketing, sales, pricing and channel distribution. Private label are only available from chosen retailer(s).

- Private label are harder to benchmark by competitors – Private labels are highly customized. This makes it hard for competitors to benchmark and undercut your price.

- Direct dealing from source - Middlemen are avoided unlike sourcing from wholesalers. You are able to get the product directly from manufacturer or dealer.

- Sense of ownership – A private label is your own brand name. No one else owns it besides you. Amazon and such other outlets only sell on your behalf.

- Private label brands are often cheaper to make than national (or international) brands. This is because the overhead costs are lower.

- Higher levels of customers' need satisfaction – it is easy to customize products under private label to suit customers' specific needs

- Value addition – with a private label, it is possible to consider that critical value that a specific niche requires and enhance it

Things to consider before choosing a private label supplier

- Check out for high quality, low price manufacturers – you are in business to make profit. You also would like to maintain customer loyalty in the long-term. Lower cost means higher profit margin. However, it is high quality that attracts customer loyalty. Thus, start by setting the quality standard you want. From that quality standard, look out for the cheapest supplier at your set standard.

- Invest in great design – Most products are actually of same key ingredients. What makes people prefer one brand over the other is the differentiation. A great design will differentiate your product from the others that have just standard design.

- Boost your channel network – Amazon marketplace is a global marketplace. You are expected to deliver in huge volumes, with short delivery times. Thus, you have to boost your production and delivery capacity. You must marshal efforts of product designers, manufacturers, and logistics providers so that they operate in synergy as a one coherent system. If you can't consider yourself capable of dealing with this, you can hire a team of consultants to carry out this work on your behalf.

- Employ pricing strategy based on market intelligence – It is easier to peg your private label to existing competitor brands. However, retailers make certain other considerations when it comes to stocking and pricing your brand. Reviews, traffic (web traffic), and ratings are signals that inform retailers' consideration to your product's price. Most significant consideration is the conversion rate. Traffic can be high, but, if conversions are low compared to competitors, that's a negative signal that might turn retailers (including Amazon) away from your listing. Thus, you have to gather this market intelligence faster than others and use it appropriately to adjust your pricing strategy.

- Take cognizance of product feature category – Consumers do look for certain features within a specific quality subset. For example, a consumer who has to choose one of two quality competitor brands of fridges will focus on what unique or extra feature that a certain brand offers in relation to the other. If each brand has a pack of unique features, the consumer will be looking at trade-offs – that is "what feature will I sacrifice in order to get the other?" The brand that has what can be sacrificed will lose in favor of that brand which has that which cannot be sacrificed. Thus, you need to have this information regarding consumer tastes, preferences and behaviors so that you establish a label which has more of those "must-have" features.

- Invest in data-driven algorithmic pricing strategy – There is nothing as challenging as pricing in a highly volatile and dynamic market. In modern times, consumers' tastes and preferences are changing quite fast. Thus, you need to invest in systems that provide you with real-time trends about changing consumer tastes and preferences. There are many specialist consultants in big data market that you can engage with to help you carry out this algorithmic pricing strategy. FBA tools are a great option to start with.

What you need to do to ensure success of your private label

- **Collaboration and partnership** – collaborate and partner with strategic marketers

- **Consumer research** – carry out in-depth consumer research to understand their attitudes, tastes and preferences

- **Collaborate to setup market-driven inventory management** – collaborate to create market-driven inventory management programs that optimizes inventory based on unique needs of the target consumer segment

- **Have highly skilled and specialized staff to handle your product** – it is not easy to have such a skilled specialized team when you are a starter. This is where Amazon FBA comes in.

- **Take advantage of technology** – 3D printing, delivery drones are emerging as newer ways of dealing with manufacturing and logistics, respectively.

When you leverage Amazon FBA you are able to achieve most of these needs. That's the great benefit of having Amazon FBA. They provide the logistics, inventory management, customer service and a pool of skilled staff to deal with virtually every other complex situation. With creativity, you can gain a lot about consumer insight by carrying out consumer research on Amazon itself. Amazon is a first-hand strategic partner via its FBA program. Nonetheless, you also need to carry out consumer research and strategic marketing beyond Amazon for you to register great success. This shouldn't be scary for a starter as one can learn and advance from experience.

Why Amazon FBA and Private Labeling makes such a perfect combination?

The reason most people go for private labeling is that they don't want to do the entire manufacturing and production process on their own. They are simply merchant traders who interested in having a brand by their name without undertaking the strenuous effort of production.

Another reason why people go for Amazon FBA is that they don't want to go through the difficult work of receiving, processing and delivery of Orders in addition to marketing, advertising, billing and claiming payment.

Thus, Amazon FBA plus private labeling automates the entire process from manufacturing/production to marketing, processing orders, delivery, billing and invoicing (payment claim). This leaves the merchant with only the creative part of generating ideas of new products to be privately labeled. Even this too can be automated. You can hire consultants to do that on your part. All you need to focus on is your earnings account. From your earnings account, you can let money work for you towards achieving your passive income goals.

Amazon FBA plus Private Labeling equals automation. This is the hassle-free intelligent way of conducting modern ecommerce. You let the money work for you as opposed to slaving yourself working for money.

Important tips to help you grow and scale your FBA business

- **Be passionate:** When you have passion for what you are doing, even when times are lean, you won't give up. You will keep going. Thus, for a start, find products that interest and excite you. Go for that niche you are passionate about. This will keep you going while you learn and discover more.

- **Diversify your product portfolio:** Every investor knows that diversification helps to reduce risks of failure. Some products are seasonal. Some are just picking up while others are ageing out. Thus, with one product, you may be discouraged when you start it out off-season or when it is just new in the market. However, if you have some other products that are on-season or already matured in the market, they help ensure that you continue having stable income flows.

- **Boost your Best Sellers Rank (BSR):** There is nothing as important as reputation. With great reputation comes Goodwill. Goodwill is that benefit you derive from customers due to your reputation. This can keep you in the market while others fall. You can ride on Goodwill to introduce new products and customers would be willing to experiment (simply because they trust you!). This can greatly help you in your diversification endeavor. All you need is availing a need-satisfying product. A need-satisfying product is that product which not only meets customer's wants but also their needs (utility). Wants (desires) do change more frequently than needs. Utility refers to a product being able to satisfy a customer because it is at the right place (delivery), at the right time and in the right form (quality, quantity, package, etc).

- **Build your niche website:** Consider Amazon as store which you have to direct customers to. Like the traditional brick-and-mortar store, there are those regular customers who know the store and there are those new customers who have been directed to the store via a sign post or inquiries. The same concept applies to ecommerce stores such as Amazon. While there are customers who know where to get Amazon online, there are those who don't. Even for those who know, they may not exactly know that a certain product can be obtained from Amazon, especially from you! There are still others who don't even know what product can satisfy their wants and needs. Only an in-depth description of the product purpose, usage and features (which cannot be fully rendered on Amazon due to space limitation) can make them realize that this is the need-satisfying product that they have been looking for. Your niche or brand website serves as this electronic sign post directing customers to your Amazon store. It also serves as your potential customer's product discovery center where the product purpose and features are described in detail so as to arouse a want (trigger demand) in the potential customer's mind. With proper SEO, your website responds to search inquiries from potential customers on the web who want a certain kind of product but they simply don't know where to get it. They Google out and your site come up with leading information regarding the product they are looking for. They click on the link from the search engine results and are led to your website. Your website displays the product plus its features and prompts the customer to get them on Amazon store via a clickable link to the product page. Building your niche website is a necessity that should be your top priority.

- **Enroll as an Amazon Associate:** Who pays you for your marketing effort? Yes, it is your product, but, aren't you worth earning for your marketing effort? The smartest thing about Amazon is that you can earn a commission marketing your very own product. You simply need to enroll with Amazon Associate program. Use your niche website to create referral links to your product page. You earn a commission for every successful buyer of your product you have referred to via your niche website. What a great way to motivate you to market your very own product! You can also establish a blog, Facebook page, Pinterest and StumbleUpon and such other social media forums where you write about your product and refer potential customers to your Amazon product page (obviously via Amazon referral link). It is fun. It is rewarding.

- **Take advantage of technology** – There are many third party FBA tools that can help you automate most of the things you would be expected to do to scale up your Amazon business and boost your passive income streams. Do take advantage of them to automate your process.

Your six figure earning potential

Amazon FBA and Private Labeling are about working smart. Every bit of smart effort is rewarded. What you earn depends on how creative you've endeavored in your smart effort. Just as smart effort is not standard, the earnings too are not standard. It all depends on your creativity. However, you can easily gauge your potential by comparing yourself with other starters who employed their smart effort in this business.

The founder of UpFuel, Chris Guthrie, was able to make about $3,000 within 30 days for starting his FBA business. The founder of Niche Pursuits, Spencer Haws, was able to make almost $40,000 within 30 days of starting his FBA enterprise.

Feedbackz founder, James Amazio, was able to scale up from $0 to $50,000 per month in just 8 months.

There are those who have been able to achieve 5, 6 and even 7-figure passive incomes by taking advantage of Amazon FBA and Private Labeling. You too can achieve this. It is all about channeling your creativity into smart effort. Money is essential, but, you don't need to have lots of money to achieve this. It is all about smartness. The rest of this book is about helping you develop and hone your smart effort. Creativity counts!

SETTING UP AN AMAZON SELLER ACCOUNT?

Setting up your Amazon seller account is the first step to becoming a seller on Amazon. It is, in essence, granting yourself the golden key to Amazon fortunes. They surely await you!

Getting started - Preparing to register

To be informed is to be equipped. Before you register to open up an account on Amazon, you need to get some information. The following is the key information that you need to equip yourself with to make your setup a smooth, stress-free endeavor;

- Know the essentials of a good profile

- Know what your business information should have

- Know Amazon policies

- Know the selling plans (seller categories) and the benefits-vs-tradeoff for each

- Know why you need the much-coveted "Buy Box"

- Know the kind of merchants who are likely to benefit most from selling on Amazon

Know the essentials of a good profile

There are certain basics that a good profile ought to have. The following are some of them;

- Logo – it should be an attractive logo with a width of about 120 pixels

- "About" section – this is a section that describes you as the seller. It is an opportunity to market your enterprise.

- Shipping information section – this provides information about shipping terms, including shipping duration (for FBA, Amazon provides details, e.g. for Amazon Prime customers, shipping is within 2 days)

- Return and refund section – this provides information about terms of return and refund (though, with FBA, Amazon has greater control over this).

- Privacy policy – this applies if there are any private terms needed (depending on the product niche)

Know what your business information should have

The following is the basic information required for your account setup;

- Brand name

- Legal business name

- Customer service contact – phone and email address

- Physical location from which item will be shipped (for FBA, Amazon takes full charge)

- Bank routing and account numbers

Know Amazon policies

The following are important Amazon policies that you need to acquaint yourself with;

- Prohibited seller activities and actions

- Product detail page rules

- Selling policies

- Shipping policies

- General policies and agreements

Know your selling plan (seller category) and the benefits-vs-tradeoff for each

Amazon offers two types of selling plans;

- **Individual** – this is for you, if you plan to sell fewer than 40 items per month

- **Professional** – this is for you if you plan to sell more than 40 items per month

Advantages of individual plan

- Good for startups as you only pay for what you sell (at $0.99 per item).

- Less overhead cost as you are not charged $39.99 (for professional plan) whether you sell or not

Disadvantages of individual plan

- Unlike the professional plan where you can sell in a combination of several markets (e.g. US, UK and Canada), the individual plan only allows you to sell in one market (e.g. US or UK or Canada)

- You cannot enjoy benefits of Amazon Marketplace Web Service (bulk listing and reporting tools)

- You cannot customize your shipping rates

- You cannot offer special promotion and gift wrap options (except for software, entertainment medium (Videos, DVDs and Music and books)

- You are not eligible for top placement on product details page

Advantages of professional plan

- Unlimited amount of products

- No fee per item (which is extremely expensive with large volumes)

- Opportunity for more income streams

- Enjoy benefits of Amazon Web Service (bulk listing and reporting tools)

- Offer special promotion and gift wrap options (which increases your sales, boosts customer satisfaction and increases your chances of positive reviews)

- You are eligible for top placement on product details page (which boosts your brand recognition and likely to increase sales)

Disadvantages of professional plan (for small scale beginners)

- The only disadvantage of the professional plan if you are a beginner is the fixed cost of $39.99 per month, whether you make a sale or not.

The rule of thumb for your choice of seller plan;

If you anticipate selling less than 40 items per month, go for individual plan. However, if you anticipate selling more than 40 items per month, go for professional plan. If you are a starter, it is prudent to start with individual plan and then scale up to professional plan when you are certain that your sales per month are consistently above 40 items and likely to grow.

Know why you need the much-coveted "Buy Box"

The "Buy Box" is simply an Amazon shopping cart tool that enables your customers to quickly add items to shopping list and do a quick checkout. This encourages buyers to shop for more items as they don't have to keep checking out individual item back and forth (see "How to Set Up your Listing" for more details).

Opening up your Amazon seller account

Steps;

1. Visit the registration site – <u>Amazon Seller Central</u>

2. Create a new account or use your already existing one

3. Set up your seller profile

4. Feedback

Setting up your seller profile

Amazon has provided step-by-step forms to enable you set up your seller profile. The following are the key areas of your seller profile that you will need to set;

- Account information

- Notification preferences

- Login settings

- Return settings

- Gift options

- Shipping settings

- Tax settings

- User permissions

- Your info and policy

- Fulfillment option (either FBA or FBM)

Encouraging feedback

There are hardly setup options for feedback. This is a setup done by Amazon. This is deliberately so to prevent sellers from manipulating feedback. However, you need to make effort to convince customers to leave feedback. This is where third party feedback tools become handy. For more on these tools, see the section on "Automating the process".

HOW TO CHOOSE YOUR NICHE

Choosing your niche is the first and foremost step you need to undertake in your Amazon FBA business.

The following are important things to consider before choosing your niche;

- Know your situation

- Establish criteria for your niche

Know your situation

Your very own situation determines so much on how you will approach your niche search. The following are the key scenarios that describe most of the situations which befell those who want to enter Amazon FBA business;

Scenario 1: You don't have money

This is a common scenario for most of those who are stepping out of college and want to have passive income. It could also befall those who have just lost jobs or are experiencing insolvency. Whatever the case, you can make it. One great advantage of those in this scenario is that they have one critical resource – time! All you need is to match your time and skill or special talent. This can enable you to earn towards your FBA business. You can also use your abundant time to learn so that you may increase your productivity towards your FBA venture when you finally launch it. The following are options to begin with;

- Sell your knowledge as a product – the best way to sell your knowledge is through books. Amazon kindle (for eBooks) and Createspace (for on-demand printing of hardcover books) and ACX (for audiobooks) are great ways to start off. You can either write the book yourself or outsource the writing to a ghostwriter. Ghostwriting is not too expensive. With $500 you are ready to start. You can sell the eBook on Amazon Kindle and send a copy of it for hard printing to Createspace which you can use to launch your Amazon FBA business.

- Sell your skill/talent as a product – If you have a talent for creating crafts, then, you have a very inexpensive way to start. You can make your crafts and sell via Amazon FBA.

- Sell your talent/skill as a service- if you are unable to sell your knowledge as a product or your talent/skill as a product, then, you can sell them as a service to other FBA merchants so that, with time, you can be able to use the raised funds to start your own FBA enterprise. The great thing about this is that you remain focused on FBA as you gain business skills, experience and exposure. Services that can be sold include; branding, seo, keyword research, niche website development, virtual assistant, product design, logo design, copywriting, etc. Amazon too has Amazon Service section where you can list to sell your services. However, most of them are not remote services.

If you are aggressive enough, you can raise funds for your FBA and Private Labeling business online through the following main options;

- Crowdfunding

- Angel funding

When you don't have money and you want to venture into FBA business, the best way is to start active and gradually go passive as you continue to automate your process.

Scenario 2: You are extremely passionate about a certain product category

Passion drives success. It is what brings patience and perseverance. With passion, you can win against all odds. If you are passionate about a certain product category, you can easily refine and convert it into a niche.

Scenario 3: You have an impeccable experience in a certain industry

If you have experience in a certain industry, e.g. apparel, electronics, crafts, drones, etc, this grants you a special advantage in that industry. You can use this industry as a starting point for your niche. The next thing is to find niche products to sell on Amazon.

Scenario 4: You have a large following on social media

To have a large loyal following on social media is not that easy. It means you have something special to offer to your fan base. Can you convert this offering into a brand? If it is not something that can be converted into a physical product (such as book, magazine, fashion label, jewelry, etc), what product do you think your fans would really die to have from you?

A large following on social media grants you a great marketing advantage. All you need is to curve out an FBA niche that can offer benefit to your fans. Things like T-shirts, Caps, Gift Cards, Stationery, books and such other items that can be branded in your social media name would inspire your fans to buy. The value is not so much intrinsic (the material being bought) but extrinsic (your name).

The great advantage of a large following on social media is that you can easily carry out research on what your fans would like to have from you before going ahead and launching it. You can even offer paid booking in advance just to explore. With booking, you can tell your fans that a booking has to reach a certain minimum for you to deliver; otherwise, you make a refund. You can keep on updating them on the progress of booking numbers. This way, it becomes some sort of a campaign in which your fans are participating in to make it succeed. Just make sure that it is not a high target to burn-out your fans or the items are so expensive that it requires them to make them make such a huge individual sacrifice. Things like T-shirts, caps, gift cards, stationery, books, etc are not such expensive and could inspire them to book and pay in advance. The beauty of this is that your fans are in essence financing your private label.

Scenario 5: You do have money

Lucky few have the required money to start off Private Labeling and to put up on Amazon FBA. If you are one of such lucky persons, congratulations! You are a step ahead of the rest. Let money work for you. Take advantage of FBA automation.

Scenario 6: None of the above scenarios fits you perfectly

If you happen not to be a perfect fit in either or some of the above 5 scenarios, then, you have to make a uniquely different approach – an almost ground zero approach. You have to build your foundation from scratch. It seems a lot of work but the benefit of unlimited creativity offsets all other disadvantages.

Research and idea generation through self-propelled brainstorming becomes the most critical of the initial steps;

1. Jot down your responsibilities, hobbies and interests

2. Subscribe to sources of information that align with your responsibilities, hobbies and interests e.g. newsletters, mailing lists, etc. Online email subscriptions are the quickest and most update sources of information (see "sources of product ideas" here below)

3. Compile a list of product ideas and classify them into categories

4. Pick out the most compelling category and refine into a niche

5. Make a shortlist of at most 10 product ideas

6. Do an in-depth research on products that fall within your shortlist. This research should comprise of product trends, consumer demand, pricing and profitability. You should also analyze customer reviews and professional reviews on the products.

7. Create a priority list of top-10 products based on your research.

8. Determine what you can do to differentiate the products (from the original product, e.g. rebranding), add value and improve customer satisfaction.

9. Re-evaluate your priority list of top-10 products and decide on the ones you can start off as your private labels based on your budgetary projections

10. Work to fit into the best combination of the 5 mentioned scenarios. Probably, you have some money but not enough, in which case you take it as if you have two shopping baskets to fill – the first basket fits scenario 5 and the second basket fits scenario 1. Use solutions for scenario 1 to get money to fill the second basket. Combine the baskets afterwards.

Great sources of product ideas

- Online marketplaces (Amazon, Alibaba, Global Resource) – Online marketplaces have plenty of product categories from which you can get great ideas about your prospective niche. On Amazon, the best place to start from is Amazon Best Seller list. This list comprise of best performing products in various categories and niches. Alibaba and Global Resource are also great places. Besides, EBay (Amazon competitor), is another great place to get product ideas.

- Blogs and trending sites – Niche blogs are especially great in helping you refine product ideas. Apart from niche sites, there exists trending sites such as **Kadaza** which can help you gain information about trending products and, in effect, trending consumer behavior, tastes and preferences.

- Research tools – There are many niche research tools in the market that are specifically designed to enable you to establish niche products for FBA through Private Labeling. For more information on these niches, please check on our last chapter "AUTOMATNG THE PROCESS".

- Shopping stores – make effort to frequent shopping stores. Check what most consumers are buying in any given day at any given moment. This will help you get information about some of the products that are in high demand.

- Trade shows – Trade shows are a great place to sample out products and make inquiries. You can meet many suppliers at one point dealing with a particular niche. Observing what attracts interest and attention of most show attendants can help you have a rough idea of possible niche products.

- Travelling – Travelling, more so, to places where your products of interest are in higher demand (such as US, Germany, France, Britain) or in plenty supply (such as China) can help you have a more informed hands-on knowledge which can help you sharpen your ideas. Both ends (consumer end and supplier end) are extremely important in helping you establish a niche.

HOW TO CHOOSE YOUR SUPPLIER

The key to choosing a supplier is having a product niche and a list of niche products that you want supplied.

The following steps will help you choose the right supplier and make an Order;

- Have a list of products that you want supplied

- Search for potential suppliers and manufacturers of each product

- Contact potential suppliers and manufacturers (to make inquiries – list them)

- Choose your supplier from your list of potential suppliers or manufacturers

- Ask for product sample

- Negotiate for price

- Order the product

Criteria for choosing your supplier

You have to setup criteria for choosing the right supplier well in advance to avoid being carried away by impulses. The following criteria will help you get the most deserved supplier;

- Relevance to the product niche – Check for a supplier that has products relevant to your niche

- Reputation – Vouch for supplier reputation. Customer reviews, supplier ranking, volume of sales, etc, are some of the things that can help you determine the supplier's reputation.

- Capability – Check the volume of successful orders to determine whether the supplier is capable of fulfilling your volume of order. Minimum Order Quantity (MOQ) stipulated by the supplier can also help you determine the supplier capacity

- Cost (price plus shipping and insurance)

- Ordering terms (minimum order quantity, batch quantities, order processing time, etc)

- Delivery/shipping terms (on spot, shipping, etc)

- Payment terms (down payment, escrow, payment in advance, etc)

- Proximity to Amazon pre-fulfillment centers

Where to source supplier info

The following are major marketplaces where you can find potential suppliers.

- Alibaba

- Global sources

- Aliexpress

- Made-In-China

- HKTDC

Alibaba seems to be the most cited by many as the best source of suppliers of Private Labels for FBA business.

HOW TO SETUP YOUR LISTING

Listing your products on Amazon is like setting up a storefront in the traditional brick-and-mortar business. The key purpose of listing is to enable buyers access your product and drive sales.

Listing on Amazon naturally comes after setting up your Amazon seller account and determining your niche products to sell.

How you list your product depends on the following factors;

- Whether you are rendering FBA (Fulfillment by Amazon or FBM(Fulfillment By Merchant)

- Whether your seller plan is individual or professional

- Whether you are directly using Amazon listing tool or third party listing tool

- Whether you are listing an already existing product or a new product

Listing sections/components

Major components of your listing include;

- Product title

- Product category

- Product description

- Product image

- Product price

- Buy box (automatically created by Amazon based upon your product meeting certain performance criteria)

Product title

Product titles on Amazon are descriptive in nature. They are kind of descriptive summary of your product in 250 words or less (Amazon keep changing this limit, confirm the current limit).

A good product title should;

- describe your product as concisely as possible (including product features and purpose)

- be Amazon SEO optimized (see "Keyword Optimization of Your Listing")

Product category

Product category determines how Amazon groups your product so as to improve searcheability. Amazon has a list of categories from which you will have to choose from through the dropdown option. Make sure that you select the right category for your product. The category must be relevant to your product niche.

Product description

The purpose of product description is to inform your customer about your product in such a manner that helps them to make a buy decision.

A good product description should;

- Be formatted in bullet form to enable easy reading by customer
- Capture salient features of your product
- Show how the customer will benefit from the product
- Inspire the customer to make a buy decision

Product image

It doesn't need to be overemphasized that the first thing that captures your potential customers' eyes on your product listing is the product image. Thus, a product image will determine whether a potential customer's attention will be captured enough to read the title and description or move on.

A good product image should;

- Have not less than 1000 pixels on the longest side (to optimize zooming). Amazon requires the image to be at least 500x500 pixels. However, for ideal zooming, you should have at least 1000x1000 pixels

- Have products filling at least 85% of the image space/dimensions

- have Amazon SEO optimized name

- be on pure white background

- have no watermarks

- have no frame borders

Amazon allows up to 9 different images of the same product. Capture different images each describing a unique feature or function or usage of your product

Product price

After the photo and title, most buyers look out for your product price before going further to read the product description. Logically, if they can't afford your product, why labor to read its description? Thus, you have to employ the right pricing strategy for your product. There are two price entries;

- Listing price (recommended price) – this is seller's guide price

- Selling price (actual price) – this is the price that the customer is eventually asked to pay by the seller

To attract buyer attention, make the actual price slightly lower than the recommended price. This will create an impression of a discount (Recommended price – Actual price). This is a good penetration pricing strategy for new entrants.

Buy box

Buy box is a tool (shopping cart box) provided by Amazon on your listing so as to quicken the checkout process. The buy box is not guaranteed by Amazon and its placement on your listing depends Amazon's own criteria. This criteria include;

- Good performance of your product (high sales volumes)

- Good pricing
- Good customer experience (positive customer reviews)
- Adherance to Amazon policy
- Several other factors (depending on Amazon metrics and algorithm)

How to list a product

Amazon Seller Central has walkthrough forms that can enable you to easily list your product. However, the following are key steps in the process of listing your product;

Step 1: Once logged in to your <u>Seller Central Account,</u> click on "Add a Product" under the inventory dropdown menu

Step 2: On the "Add a Product" page, click on "create a new product listing" appearing immediately below the search bar

Step 3: Assign your new product to Amazon category

Step 4: Fill in the listing details under Vital Info Tab (in the next page that comes after step 3). These listing details include;

- Product name
- Manufacturer and brand name (for private label, you can fill brand name in both spaces)
- Manufacturer Part Number (you can leave blank if not relevant)
- Etc

There are many details to fill out. You can skip out those not relevant to your product

Step 5: Fill in information in other Tabs including;

- Variations Tab

- Offer Tab

- Images Tab

- Description Tab

- Keywords Tab

- More Details Tab

Step 6: Save and Finish

Your product is now listed!

KEYWORD OPTIMIZATION OF YOUR LISTING

Keyword optimization is extremely critical to the performance of your listing on Amazon. It will determine how fast your income streams flow. Obviously, to achieve a 6-figure passive income, this rate of flow must be high.

To optimize your keywords so as to achieve a 6-figure passive income requires you to master the following;

1. Understanding of Amazon's algorithm

2. Keyword research

3. Click-Through Rate (CTR) factors

4. Conversion rate factors

5. Sales as a an optimization factor

Understanding Amazon's Algorithm

To optimize an engine, you have to master how it operates. This is the same rationale for Search Engine Optimization (SEO). Amazon search engine is no exception. Amazon SEO uses what is popularly referred to as A9 algorithm. This is the algorithm they use to rank products in the search results. With this understanding, you can find and use keywords that can optimize your listing SEO. This will put you one step ahead of the pack.

The key philosophy of Amazon's A9 algorithm is to increase the likelihood of a customer making a purchase. Thus, unlike Google, Bing or Yahoo, Amazon algorithm is about nothing else but BUYING! Like Google, Bing, Yahoo and other search engines, most people searching online will consider the first page (mostly, the first 10 items) on the SERP (Search Engine Results Page). Thus, you effort should be geared towards your listing/products appearing on the first SERP. If it can appear among the top 3 items, there is a great likelihood that the link leading to your listing will be clicked.

The following are key factors considered by Amazon's A9 algorithm when it comes to ranking;

- **Relevance factors** – This refers to how well the product listing matches the search query. Relevance is mainly computed based on how the keyword is used and how it is positioned (e.g. in the title, first description paragraph, etc)

- **Performance factors** – This refers to how the product has performed in terms of popularity and success. The three critical performance indicators are; Click-Through Rate (CTR), Conversion Rate (CR) and Sales Turnover (ST). Of course, the most rational ranking priority is ST followed by CR and finally CTR. However, it is CTR that gives birth to CR. CR boosts the chances of ST occurring or increasing. It is also important to note that CTR depends heavily on relevance factors (Amazon SEO).

It is important to observe that relevance factors (which are mostly within your control and which you can greatly influence through SEO) directly and indirectly drives performance factors (which you may not have great leeway to influence). Nonetheless, product quality, branding, pricing, promotion and customer support are factors within your control and which you can tune to greatly improve your performance and drive ST.

How to carry out thorough keyword research

Keyword research (KR) is the bedrock of SEO. Without KR, your SEO effort is a blind, primitive guesswork. What is keyword research? Keyword research involves finding all relevant keywords for your product that would enable it to be easily searchable. The most important approach in keyword research is to put yourself in the customer's shoes. In this regard, you ask yourself, "Which kind of words would I type on the search bar if I wanted to find a certain kind of product that I need? Thus, SEO keywords are simply keywords that a customer would most likely use to search for your product.

Types of keywords

There are basically two types of keywords:

- Short-tail keywords

- Long-tail keywords

Short-tail keywords

Also known as "head" or "term" keywords, they comprise of 1 to 3 words. There are two types of short-tail keywords;

- Primary keywords – these are keywords that are specific to the product's core essence. This includes its identification and description. For example "jogging shoes".

- Secondary keywords – these are keywords that associate the primary keywords to a target group, event, season, time, circumstance/situation, function, size, shape, appearance, material, place, etc. For example, secondary keywords associated with "jogging shoes" could be; target group: "children jogging shoes", "male jogging shoes", "female jogging shoes"; event: "Halloween jogging shoes"; season: "winter jogging shoes", "summer jogging shoes"; etc.

Long-tail keywords

Long-tail keywords are those keywords (usually three or more words) that are more specific to meeting a certain need or providing a certain solution.

SEO features of long-tail keywords;

- They have low competition

- They have low search rate

Advantages of long-tail keywords

- They have high conversion rate – most serious searchers are specific about what they are looking for and thus they are more likely to buy an item should they find it. For example, if you are selling tour packages for Mount Everest then "Mount Everest" will bring over 1000 visitors per day. However most of the visitors probably are geography students or those who just want to get general information about Mount Everest. Very few are interested in tour package – probably 5. On the other hand, if you use "Mount Everest climbing tour package", only serious persons would type such on their search bar. Probably, out of 80 visitors, 15 of them will buy the package. Thus, though there is less competition for long-tail keywords (low search rate) there is higher conversion rate.

- Since long-tail keywords have less competition, their CPC (Cost per Click) rate is low. This means that you will use less advertising budget.

Click-Through Rate (CTR) factors

Click-Through Rate refers to the ratio of the number of people who click on an advert against the number of people who view the advert.

Factors determining Click-Through Rate are;

- Brand name – an attractive brand name will more likely excite a potential customer to click so as to know what the brand is all about

- Title – a great title will compel a potential customer to want to know what your product is all about

- Image – an optimized image creates a great impression about a product thus raising interest and curiosity

- Price – a price that seems too good will raise potential customer's curiosity to find out more

- Bestseller /Amazon Choice label – Bestseller or Amazon choice label raises potential customer's trust about your product. This makes the potential customer feel confident to click on the link to your product.

Conversion Rate factors

Conversion refers to the act of converting site visitors into buying customers. Conversion rate refers to the number of conversions per click (ad click). Conversion rate is computed by dividing the number of conversions against the number of clicks.

The following are key factors that determine conversion rate;

- Image – An optimized image creates an impression about your product's quality, need-satisfaction, and fitness for purpose among other impressions that compel a potential customer to give your product a try.

- Reviews – Reviews are about reputation. Positive reviews increase your product reputation. Thus, a potential customer asks "If all these customers are happy and satisfied about this product, why not me?" This boosts the customer's confidence to buy your product.

- Description format (bullet points) – When it comes to description, it is not just a matter of compelling description but also presentation. Many customers are easily worn out after going through dozens of listings to arrive at your listing. A poor presentation will discourage them from reading your description hence fail to buy your product. A bullet point presentation makes it easy for a customer to read as the key points are summarized. This too motivates a quick buying decision.

Sales as an optimization factor

Amazon pride itself in products that increase its revenue. Thus, if your product performs well, Amazon will list it into prominent categories such as Bestseller, Popular, Most Liked (high number of positive reviews), etc. These are unique ways by which Amazon is marketing your product and granting it more exposure to customers. All you need to do is to make sure that your product performs so that you can benefit from this free publicity by Amazon.

How to optimize your listing content

You have to do keyword optimization of every part of your listing content including title, price (captured by Amazon price metrics), photos, product description, search terms (most likely used by buyers to search for items).

Optimizing product title

To optimize your title, it should;

- Be less than 150 characters

- Concisely describe your product

- Be grammatically correct

- Contain your brand name

- Have 3 SEO keywords

Also, consider registering your brand with Amazon Brand Registry

Optimizing price

To optimize price;

- Set higher list price and lower sale price. The difference represents a discount that would attract customers to benefit from.

(Though, Amazon seems to be interested in phasing out this option due to persistent abuse by sellers e.g. exaggerating list price to appear to be offering great discounts).

Optimizing photos

- Save using names with SEO keywords but each photo must have a unique name

Optimizing Product description

1. Incorporate both short-tail and long-tail keywords

2. Consider applying for Amazon's Enhanced Brand Content

Optimizing Search Terms

- Use secondary keywords – at least 5 of them

Optimizing via Keywords from Amazon PPC

- Subscribe for Amazon PPC advertisement

A Short message from the Author:

Hey, are you enjoying the book? I'd love to hear your thoughts!

Many readers do not know how hard reviews are to come by, and how much they help an author.

I would be incredibly thankful if you could take just 60 seconds to write a brief review on Amazon, even if it's just a few sentences!

Please head to the product page, and leave a review as shown below.

Thank you for taking the time to share your thoughts! Your review will genuinely make a difference for me and help gain exposure for my work.

BRANDING YOUR PRODUCTS

Branding refers to the process of deliberately creating a unique impression of a given product so as to create a certain desired value in the mind of the consumer.

Brand development

In branding your product, you must remember that it is an integral part of marketing. Thus, it must integrate well with other components of marketing. The 8Ps of Marketing are the key components that your branding must take cognizance of. Your brand must mirror (reflect) all these 8Ps.

The 8Ps of marketing;

- **Product** – a product is a unit (item) that has both intrinsic (good or object with shape and dimensions) and extrinsic (idea, information, method, service) attributes with a certain need- or want-satisfying value (features, functions, uses, benefits) that the seller offers to the buyer for a price. You can see that there is so much in a product other than its physical attributes. Branding not only serves to accentuate the physical attributes (through shape, color, texture, etc) but also create a certain desired impression (idea, information, service, solution, and need-satisfaction) in the mind of the buyer such as to trigger a purchase action.

- **Price** – Price subtly communicates the worth of a product. It represents what the seller expects the buyer to sacrifice in order to gain need- or want-satisfying value. The price should create an impression that the buyer is sacrificing less than the value to be received. For example, this is why most sellers quote a price minus 1 cent e.g. $0.99 instead of $1, $39.99 instead of $40 and so on. A buyer is more likely going to buy a product priced at $0.99 instead of $1 and $39.99 instead of $40. Why? Because, the sacrifice is "less than" what it ought to be, though, the difference is so negligible and there no possibility of a balance being returned if the same were to be bought in a traditional brick-and-mortar shop. However, the impact of this one-cent difference in consumer psychology is so profound.

- **Place** – Place represents all attributes relating to the delivery space. This delivery space could be virtual (online) or physical (where the customer picks up the product). This space also includes the environment – cleanliness, orderliness, organization, ambience, etc. The place ought to reflect both intrinsic and extrinsic attributes that you intend to be perceived by the customer. A dirty, disorderly, disorganized place represents low value and poor quality product. Place with an ambience that is classy, relaxed, homely and welcoming makes the customer feel at ease thus triggering a sense of higher value.

- **Promotion** – Promotion refers to all efforts geared towards facilitating sales. In the mind of the buyer, promotion makes the buyer feel wanted, welcomed and appreciated. However, promotion shouldn't be aggressive enough to invade buyer's privacy or right to decide as this can have negative effect.

- **People** – How people (staff) interact with one another, how they carry out their work, how they render customer service, etc. creates a certain impression in the mind of the customer. Poor staff interaction (quarrelling, snubbing, shouting, etc), slow delivery, erratic work patterns and poor customer service (lack of attention, lack of courtesy, negative body language, etc) are all signs of a poor brand.

- **Process** – Process refers to all those activities geared towards delivering value to the consumer. This include shipping, delivery and after-sales service (if any, and ought to be created if customer loyalty has to be achieved). A great process increases the worth of your brand.

- **Performance** – This is about productivity. How the company acts as a steward of resources – e.g. optimizing utility in an environment-friendly manner; respect for employees and fair remuneration; corporate social responsibility, etc. Branding should be such as to show that there is concern for this.

- **Positioning** – This is how the seller wants to be considered in the mind of the public as uniquely different from other sellers (e.g. industry leader in a certain dimension). The brand should be able to achieve this in the mind of its key publics (including buyers).

Brand identity (product)

Brand identity is about differentiating your brand from others. The following are things you need to do in order to have brand identity;

- Create a brand name – The brand name should relate to your niche rather than your product. A brand name base on your product is limiting as you cannot diversify your income streams by having different products within the niche using the same brand name.

- Create logo – A logo creates a unique impression in the mind of the buyer thus enabling the buyer to easily identify your products and distinguish them competitors' products

- Create trademark – A trademark is simply a unique mark that identifies a particular product.

- Create package design – Salt is salt. Sugar is sugar. How does one differentiate salt or sugar from different sellers? Packaging! With a special packaging (including shape, quantity, size, dimensions, shape, color, etc) helps the consumer to differentiate your product from those of competitors.

Brand value/measurability (price)

Pricing depends on the buyer's perceived value. Some products fetch a higher price than others despite having the same intrinsic value. This is because of how seller has managed to create an impression in the buyers minds about their higher value.

Brand deliverability (place)

Consumers get satisfaction when a brand is within reach of meeting their needs and wants. These channels of distribution and delivery time are unique attributes that can distinguish a brand from the rest.

Brand recognition (promotion)

Brand recognition refers to activities and processes engaged in making the brand get recognized by target customers. Brand recognition involves publicity and promotion.

Publicity

- Niche website

- Press releases

- Public relations

- Advertisement

- Product/niche directory listing

Promotion

- Free samples

- Gifts

- Free eBooks

- Free user training

Brand sensitivity (people)

- Train customer staff to deliver great service

- Interact via social media

- Respond to feedbacks

- Factor in consumer psychology

Brand activity (process)

- Productivity

- Economy (efficiency and effectiveness)

- Turnover

Brand performance (performance)

- Performance measurement – infographics

- Consumer satisfaction

- Market response (recognition and improved sales)

- Customer loyalty (Goodwill)

- Customer reviews (on Amazon, Yelp, etc)

- Profitability

Amazon Brand Registry (ABR) – this is optional

The best way to claim and prove ownership of your brand on Amazon is to register it at Amazon Brand Registry.

Eligibility

Sellers eligible for Amazon Brand Registry are those who either;

- Are traditional manufacturers

- Make their own products

- Own a private label

- Produce branded white label products

- Are distributors with express permission from manufactures to own a brand's content on Amazon

Prerequisites

- Working website

- Official email

- Product/package images

- Unique identifier (e.g. UPC, EAN, JAN, Model No., Manufacturer Part No., Catalog No., etc)

Benefits

- Brand protection

- Enhanced control over listing

Amazon's Enhanced Brand Content (EBC) – this is optional

Amazon's EBC is a more standardized, professional and premium (yet free) way of placing brand content on your listing so that it is more effectively exposed by Amazon system to potential buyers.

The following are the benefits of applying Amazon's EBC;

- Enhanced content formatting options e.g. headings, subheadings, sections, paragraphs, bold, italics, bullets, underline, etc.

- Usage of sections to enhance logical flow of content

- Better visual effects as images can be placed inside description

- Content becomes easier to scan by readers for faster reading

DRIVING TRAFFIC AND GETTING INITIAL REVIEWS

Your listing is like a center and Amazon the city within which that center is found. There are many channels flowing into and through Amazon and some of them to your center. To increase the traffic flow to your center, you have to create more feeder channels from the main channels into your center. This is where Amazon SEO comes in. However, this is simply the inner traffic. Thus, how much traffic will flow into your center will depend on the inner traffic. What if the existing inner traffic is not sufficient?

If the inner traffic is not sufficient, then, you will have to attract outer traffic into the inner traffic. This traffic will come from sources outside Amazon ecosystem. Hence, we have two main sources of traffic to your listing;

- Amazon ecosystem

- Beyond Amazon ecosystem

Driving traffic from Amazon ecosystem into your listing

Driving traffic from Amazon ecosystem into your listing encompasses the following;

- Amazon SEO – we have already covered this under Keyword optimization of your listing (see KEYWORD OPTIMIZATION OF YOUR LISTING)

- Choose the right fulfillment option – studies have indicated that Amazon algorithm tends to give preference to FBA (Fulfillment by Amazon) over FBM (Fulfillment by Merchant). Thus, if you are dealing with the same product under the two options, the product under FBA option will rank higher on the SERP (Search Engine Result Page), other things remaining the same.

- Focus on getting quality positive reviews (through promotion, great product and service) – Positive reviews are largely related to successful sales and great customer experience. They are a premium quality of your sales turnover (ST). The higher the volume of positive reviews the greater is the performance of your listing. Amazon definitely wants to generate more revenue and would naturally give priority to a product that is generating more sales. Thus, your ranking will get higher and definitely more traffic flow to your listing. Don't forget that Bestseller is not just about your product registering big volume of sales, but big volume of sales compared to similar products from your competitor.

Driving traffic beyond Amazon ecosystem into your listing

The following are ways by which you can drive traffic from beyond Amazon ecosystem;

- Non-Amazon SEO – driving traffic from beyond Amazon will require you to device a different approach to SEO targeting popular search engines including Google, Bing, Yahoo, among others. This is mainly done through content marketing.

- Directory listing – there are many directories offering niche placements and contact details. Providing these with links to your Amazon product page is the best way to utilize directory listing to drive traffic to your listing.

- Social Media activity – it is estimated that over 2 billion people are actively on social media. Thus, using social media can be a great means of driving traffic to your listing. For example, you can open a Facebook page for your niche and post content with links to your Amazon listing. You can use Twitter to provide news about your new product launch or enhanced features or versions of your existing product. You can use Pinterest to show photos of your newly launched products. StumbleUpon is a great social media for new product discovery. You simply don't forget to link your social media activity to your Amazon listing.

- Videos – Videos have the most magnetic attraction with the millennial generation. If your products are targeting millennials, then, creating "how-to" videos is the best way to attract them to your Amazon listing. Make a great "how-to" video about your product, upload on YouTube and simply link it to your Amazon listing.

- Press Releases (PR) – There are several PR sites where you can launch your press release. Though reputable PR sites are difficult to list on (due to high standard of quality expected), once successful, you can get a huge volume of traffic to your site.

- Advertisement (PPC) – Pay per Click (PPC) is the most popular form of online advertising. The Google empire is heavily reliant on PPC advertisement. Facebook too offers PPC advertisement. There are many others, but, these are the leaders. Simply create an advert (text, image, animation, video or a combination of some or all of these) as per the advertising platform requirements. Pay and upload the advert and let the advertising platform launch it to your target audience. Whenever potential customers click the advert, they are directed to your product listing.

- Niche Website – a niche website is a website specifically designed and developed to provide content and promote activities related to your niche products. This is a must-have if you intent increase your passive income streams.

Advantages of owning niche website as a tool for driving traffic

Niche website has advantages over other advertising media discussed above. The following are some of the advantages;

- It is cheaper in the long-term – once you have created a niche website, all you need to pay is hosting. If you aren't busy, you can easily run your niche website, more so, if it is a CMS (Content Management System) such as WordPress, Drupal, Joomla, among others. So far, WordPress is the most popular CMS to use to develop your niche website. It is so simple such that you can actually build it yourself.

- You own your content – when it comes to online marketing, content is king. To own your content, you have to self-host your niche website. There are plenty of online platforms such as Blogger, WordPress.org (as opposed to WordPress.com) and others which provide you with a website where you load content. You don't spend money to create the website. Neither do you spend money to host. It is "free!" Really? In real sense, there a cost – your content. When you provide your content to such "free" websites, you forfeit your right to it. The content ceases to belong to you. The provider of this "free" website uses it as a source of advertisement revenue – earning at your sacrifice!

- You can optimize on structural SEO – SEO is not just about content. It is also about the "container" that holds the content and channels (links) that draw out information from it. SEO-friendly programming requires that you use programming language that is friendly to search engines (such as HTML) as opposed to programming language that is not SEO-friendly (such as JavaScript). Links to content should also flow without breakage (or obstruction) so that the content can easily be accessed, flow and be fetched by the search engines. Links are broken when they are not associated with any content (i.e. linked to a deleted page, removed video, removed page, etc). Links are obstructed if the search engines cannot access the content being linked to (due to usage of non-SEO-friendly language). Having pages that are not linked creates redundant inaccessible "islands" of content.

- You can place your own advertisements on the website for free – you don't have to pay anyone to advertise on your niche website. Amazon has widgets that enables you advertise products (including your products) on your website.

- You can advertise your website just as you would advertise your product – Your content is a product! The more it is consumed the more likely its consumers will be interested in consuming what it refers to – your products. Thus, it makes great sense to advertise your niche website.

- You can provide more information on your niche website about your product which you couldn't provide in your listing – Unlike your listing on Amazon, there is no space limitation when it comes to your niche website. You can give detailed product features, user instructions, demonstration videos, animation graphics, offer promotional materials (downloads, free samples, gifts, etc – which you can't possibly do on Amazon when you have individual seller plan).

- You can easily market your niche in the listing directories – most listing directories don't entertain content that solicit customers (i.e. sales pitch content). This makes it impossible to link your Amazon listing on them. However, you can link to your niche site page provided that the link targets content that is not sales-pitched in nature. The good thing is that you can place your adverts on the page just as Google and other advertising media does.

Getting initial reviews

Getting initial reviews requires good work. There are no tricks to getting genuine positive reviews for your product.

The following are some of the things that can bring forth initial positive reviews

- Great listing – A listing that is professional (good photo, proper title, helpful description, etc) will create a positive impression in the customers mind and will obviously prompt for a reward in terms of positive review.

- Product quality – Quality product means customer satisfaction. Make sure that the product is of good quality but also meets customers' expectations as described. Thus, don't exaggerate customer expectations. Be honest with what the customer is expected to get.

- Proper pricing – Price represents the sacrifice that the customer makes to receive the value of your product. If the customer feels that the sacrifice (price) is abnormally higher than the value (product quality), then, negative reviews are likely. However, if customers are satisfied that they have received value for their money, then, positive reviews are more likely.

- Good inventory management – There is nothing frustrating like when customers miss product they want due to stock outs (especially loyal customers). This will negate their Goodwill and thus reduce the likelihood of a 5-star review. Ensuring that product is available when needed is improves customer satisfaction. This can be achieved through good inventory management.

Also, make sure you follow up with customers after they purchase the product; and request a review.

AUTOMATING THE PROCESS

Automating Amazon FBA and Private Labeling is the fastest way to Build a Six Figure Passive Income Streams.

Processes that you can automate

The following are the processes that you can easily automate and whose automation tools we are going to discuss;

- Niche search – Niche search is the most critical of all FBA processes. It is the foundation and source of your passive income streams. Thus, it is the process that needs quality focus and attention. Yet, it is the most encompassing process as one has to sieve through hundreds of thousands of products just to get the high value FBA 'gems'. It is some sort of data mining in its own regard. Niche search cannot be effective and efficient without the help of niche search tools.

- Product selection – Once you have established a niche, the next thing is to select products within that niche that optimizes your income streams. In this regard, you need to carry out analysis of product cost versus its profitability without forgetting that profit maximization also depends on volumes (demand). Product selection tools help you get high-yielding products (based on customer demand) that optimize your income streams.

- Private labeling – Private labeling is the supply side of FBA. Once you have established the right product, you need to convert them into private labels that can hit the market. The crux of private labeling is getting the right supplier. In this regard, product quality standardization (for comparison amongst various suppliers, cost-effectiveness, production capacity and delivery logistics) are of utmost importance. There are several Private Labeling tools that can greatly assist you in this process so that you can be able to make an informed decision (choice).

- Listing – Listing is more about stocking and presenting your merchandize to the Amazon marketplace. Like any traditional brick-and-mortar shop, the importance of organized attention-capturing display cannot be forsaken. What captures customers' attention attracts money. However great your product is, poor listing will repel money away thus suppressing your income streams. Listing tools are great in helping you have the best listing possible.

- Inventory management – Having excessive or redundant stock ties your capital thus limiting your income generating options. On the other hand, stock outs due to inadequate inventory makes you miss on potential incomes, frustrate your customers and attracts negative Goodwill. Having no stock is the other language of telling a potential customer "I don't need your money now, please try elsewhere". The best trick is to have optimal stock level. However, in a huge, delicate and dynamic market such as Amazon marketplace, you cannot be certain about the most optimal stock level as the market dynamics are extremely fluid. Thus, you need inventory management tools that are critically sensitive and respond efficiently and effectively to the rapidly changing dynamics. At the bare minimum, such tools should be able to forecast the market, predict scenarios, determine minimum stock level, re-order level, re-order quantity and maximum stock level as per the forecast and most likely scenario.

- Consumer insight (consumer metrics) – Big data has become the inevitable reality of global commerce. The volume of data that flow in a day in a global market such as Amazon would require you to employ thousands of pen-and-paper analysts. Luckily, there are Big data tools specifically tailored to help you get incisive consumer insights almost instantly. You need to be able to tell consumer trends to be able to forecast changing consumer behavior, attitudes, tastes and preferences. This is crucial for medium-term and long-term planning. This will greatly help in your product design, product branding, product lifecycle, pricing, inventory management and exploration of new niches.

- Marketing – Marketing is about all efforts geared towards availing need-satisfying/want-satisfying product to the consumer. We've seen its facets (the 8Ps) under 'BRANDING'. It is a massive effort. It is the core consumer-side (as opposed to supplier-side) effort. Whether income streams will flow or not absolutely depends on marketing. This is how critical it is. Thus, marketing tools must not be spared or laid to waste.

- Copywriting and keyword management – Copywriting and keyword management are part of the online marketing strategies. The importance of this unique management continues to grow as we advance in ecommerce. We've seen the importance of keyword optimization before. Here we are looking on how to automate it and available tools that we can use to achieve this automation.

- Customer interaction – We've seen how reviews are important in driving and maintaining traffic (potential income flows) to your listing. However, these reviews depend on how interactive you are with your customers. Building a solid goodwill depends on effective communication. Every customer's action needs a communication response from the seller. With online market such as Amazon where sales takes place 24/7 across the globe, it is not possible to achieve this without the aid of customer interaction tools that detects every customer action and responds appropriately.

- International payment – Ecommerce is global. However, the payment systems (more so, banking) remains pretty traditional (though with some online facets). Banking is subject to laws. Laws are territorial in nature. Yet ecommerce is non-territorial. It is not uncommon for international sellers to find it hard to receive money for their sales from Amazon. Major US companies (due to restrictive laws, tax requirements, global politics, and punitive government actions) demand that payments be channeled to US bank accounts (in case of US-based Amazon.com marketplace). It is without doubt that the bulk of Amazon consumers are based in US. Yet, a significant number of FBA sellers are non-US residents/citizens. Thus, they cannot receive payment without having a US bank account. Nonetheless, there are various tools that have come up to deal with this reality – to help non-US resident sellers to receive payment on Amazon.com.

There are specific FBA automation tools that you can use to automate each of the mentioned processes.

FBA Automation Tools

The following are main categories of FBA automation tools;

- Amazon FBA niche tools

- Amazon FBA Product Selection tools

- Amazon FBA Listing tools

- Amazon FBA Copywriting and Keyword management

- Amazon FBA Pricing tools

- Amazon FBA Inventory tools

- Amazon FBA Consumer Insight tools (consumer metrics)

- Amazon FBA Marketing tools

- Customer interaction tools

- Amazon FBA Payment tools

Amazon FBA niche tools

- Niche Hunter

- Niche Wolf

- Amasuite

Amazon FBA Product Selection tools

- Jungle Scout Web App

- Jungle Scout Chrome extension

- CamelCamelCamel

Amazon FBA Listing tools

- [Ecomdash](#)
- [Sellbrite](#)
- [Scanlister](#)
- [Listtee](#)

Amazon FBA Copywriting and Keyword management

- [AMZ Tracker](#)
- [MerchantWords](#)
- [Sonar](#)
- [Scientific Seller](#)
- [SeoChart](#)
- [Rank Tracker](#)
- [Google Keyword Planner](#)

Amazon FBA Pricing tools

- [Jungle Scout](#)
- [RepricerExpress](#)
- [Stitchlabs](#)
- [MarketHustl](#)

Amazon FBA Inventory tools

- [Restock](#)

- Teikametrics
- Ecomdash
- Veeqo
- Finale Inventory
- Forecastly

Amazon FBA Consumer Insight tools (consumer metrics)

- Amazooka
- AMZtracker

Amazon FBA Marketing tools

- Amazon Advertising
- Unicorn Smasher

Customer interaction & satisfaction tools

- FeedbackGenius
- Salesbacker
- Tomoson

Amazon FBA Payment tools

If you are large-scale non-US resident/citizen, you can apply to setup a US bank account to receive payments from Amazon. However, for small-scale non-US resident/citizen, this becomes expensive due international transaction costs and foreign exchange costs.

The following debit/credit cards can help you solve this challenge;

- Payoneer Debit Card – Payoneer Debit Card is MasterCard linked to a US Bank Account on your behalf. You simply need to request for this to be setup for you. You can use your Debit Card to withdraw money from MasterCard branded ATMs around the globe.

- US Unlocked Debit Card – This renders similar service as Payoneer Debit Card. However, Unlike Payoneer, you have to use a US-based shipping and billing address (which is a plus). You can use US Unlocked Debit Card to withdraw money from Visa branded ATMs worldwide.

Currency exchange is another critical issue when it comes to international transactions. Banks are known not to offer great conversion rates (thus chewing a significant bite of your hard-earned cash). If you want to exchange your currency online, the following are useful tools;

- CurrencyFair

- TransferWise

Service automation

There are certain services that go with FBA and Product Labeling. So far, we have been discussing more or less on Do-It-Yourself basis whereby you are mostly a solopreneur (carrying out business as a sole proprietor). This is probably the best starting point as a beginner. However, as your business expands and you scale up, you need helping hands. This is whereby you have to automate services that you previously provided by outsourcing them.

The following are services that you can easily outsource;

- Private labeling

- Product Design & Branding

- Listing

- Web design and development

- SEO

- Marketing

- Consumer Metrics

- Customer interactions

You can easily get workers (specialists) to carry out web design, SEO, graphics design (for branding) and marketing from freelancing sites such as <u>Upwork.com</u>, <u>Freelancer.com</u>, <u>Fiverr,</u> among others for a start. If your scale is high, you can enlist the services of established consultants in respective areas.

CONCLUSION

Thank you for acquiring this book.

It is my sincere hope that this book has not only provided relevant information but has also inspired you to start off and become a successful Amazon FBA private label entrepreneur.

Again, thank you for purchasing this book.

The end... almost!

Reviews are not easy to come by.

As an independent author with a tiny marketing budget, I rely on readers, like you, to leave a short review on Amazon.

Even if it's just a sentence or two!

So if you enjoyed the book, please head to the product page, and leave a review as shown below.

Customer Reviews

★★★★★ 2
5.0 out of 5 stars ▾

5 star		100%
4 star		0%
3 star		0%
2 star		0%

Share your thoughts with other customer

Write a customer review

I am very appreciative for your review as it truly makes a difference.

Thank you from the bottom of my heart for purchasing this book and reading it to the end.

www.ingramcontent.com/pod-product-compliance
Lightning Source LLC
Chambersburg PA
CBHW071503210326
41597CB00018B/2667